# TWELVE STEPS
# TOWARD
# POLITICAL
# REVELATION

## ALSO BY **WALTER MOSLEY**

# TWELVE STEPS TOWARD POLITICAL REVELATION

The potential for an
American epiphany under
the rough blanket of capitalism

## WALTER MOSLEY

NATION
BOOKS

New York

Published by Nation Books,
A Member of the Perseus Books Group

Nation Books is a co-publishing venture
of the Nation Institute
and the Perseus Books Group

Books published by Nation Books are available at special discounts
for bulk purchases in the United States by corporations, institutions,
and other organizations. For more information, please contact the
Special Markets Department at the Perseus Books Group, 2300
Chestnut Street, Suite 200, Philadelphia, PA 19103, or call (800)
810-4145, ext. 5000, or e-mail special.markets@perseusbooks.com.

Typeset in 11.5 point Adobe Caslon Pro

The Library of Congress has cataloged the printed edition as follows:

Mosley, Walter.
  Twelve steps toward political revelation / Walter Mosley.
      p. cm.
  ISBN 978-1-56858-642-7 (pbk. : alk. paper)—ISBN 978-1-56858-
667-0 (ebook)  1.  Political participation—United States—Hand-
books, manuals, etc.  I. Title.
  JK1764.M695 2011
  323'.0420973—dc22
                                      2011003705

10 9 8 7 6 5 4 3 2 1

FOR
ILSE "MUCK" KAHN,
WHO FOUGHT
THE REVOLUTION
FOR NINETY-SEVEN YEARS—
AND WON

# CONTENTS

# A
# PREFATORY
# NOTE

In the following pages I refer to the ranks of the wealthy-elite as *the Joes*. I dub the rich with this pedestrian appellation because I do not see them, as individuals, as being different from anyone else—aside, that is, from the size of their bank accounts. In my opinion the rich, on the whole, are regular people with nothing special to recommend them—in essence, they're just regular Joes. They have simply found their slot on the roulette of history.

Some people are wealthy, others poor; but we are all folks. The mistake Marx made in *Capital*, I believe, was to refer to the rich man as Mr. Moneybags. The intonation of this term, in small but important ways, removes the capitalist from the constructs of history that necessarily formed him just as surely as they created the poor woman, the slave, and the victims of colonization and industrialization. And so, I have degraded the name of the rich man so that we can see him as just another guy with certain privileges that he does not deserve.

# FOREWORD

This book is an exploration into the ways in which we are oppressed (along with the possibilities of overthrowing that tyranny) in our everyday lives. It is about conceiving of and implementing an intellectual revolution in this country, this land—a real revolution where power is wrenched from the hands of the ruling classes and taken into the embrace of the People as a whole.

My approach is simple. What I intend to do is explore the ways in which the systems and institutions of this nation place heavy loads and hidden addictions on our bodies and minds at the earliest possible age and then expect us to labor under these weights from childhood until the day we die. This minor treatise will also deal with the ways in which we are robbed of our wealth and then exploited by the ensuing wealthy classes with the very products of our labor and our genius. The revolution I am recommending does not call for bloodshed or physical violence of any kind. But it will require steely resolve and for us to question beliefs as powerful as the old-time certainty that the world is flat.

It is possible even today for one to prove that the world we live upon is flat. All you have to do is take a child out onto a parking lot and place a carpenter's level on the asphalt showing that the little bubble aligns perfectly—proving that the earth we walk upon is a continual plane. What argument can the child make against this claim? Even if she gazes at the sky and wonders, the proof of an imperfect sphere hurtling through space is theoretical at best and most people believe it not because of their understanding of astronomical evidence but simply because they were told.

We are told many things; some of them are true, many are not.

*I pledge allegiance to the Flag of the United States of America, and to the Republic for which*

*it stands, one Nation under God, indivisible,*
*with liberty and justice for all.*

With hand over heart I recited that thinly disguised prayer every morning in my elementary school and, later, in my junior high. I never questioned it—not once. I never doubted pledging loyalty to a flag raised too often in the name of imperialism; to a country that swears itself to the double standard of wealth and poverty; to a God that our own revolution says is up to the individual not the government; to an indivisibility that is black and white, brown and red, male and female, young and old, rich and poor, legal and illegal; to liberty in a nation founded upon slavery and genocide; and to justice where even the most conservative patriot knows that the best legal defense is a fat bank account.

We are not encouraged to question the basic lies grilled into us by rote in school. The world is round and everything else we are taught is true unless otherwise indicated.

I am an alcoholic.

For years in my late teens and early twenties I'd drink very close to a quart of whisky (or its equivalent) almost every night. I'd imbibe until I was a stumbling, mumbling drunkard—a danger to myself and to others. Twice, I almost died from *accidents* I had while inebriated. And then one night, at the bottom of a deep ravine and lucky to be alive, I realized that I had to stop drinking.

There was no heartfelt drama or deep psychological cause for my addiction(s). I didn't lose my mother at an early age; nor was I thrown into prison for a crime I didn't commit. I didn't live in poverty so dire that I had to escape into alcoholism just to face the day.

No. I drank because there was a dull but consistent pain in my heart. I wanted to shut off the feeling of hopelessness that dogged me. My television and my teachers, newspapers, and employers informed me in ways both subtle and brazen that I was never going to climb out of the rabbit-warren of my life. I was told, and I believed, that I was always going to be an underachiever navigating the slow lane, never getting much beyond the starting line of a mundane life. If I wanted to laugh or love or just look up at the stars while taking in a deep, meaningful breath I had to be three sheets to the wind with a drink in my hand.

During the same span of time, and for much the same reasons, I was a heavy cigarette smoker. I sucked down three packs of nonfiltered cigarettes every twenty-four hours. This was back in the day when you could smoke anywhere. I lit up in elevators and while sitting with my friends and their children. It was a rare moment when there wasn't a cigarette between my yellowed fingertips. I smoked in cars, classrooms, and cinemas. Once again—I was a danger to myself and to others.

These addictions, these obsessions, these all-encompassing pastimes consumed me and made me a noxious hazard.

But I was lucky: I'm just as obsessive about not doing things as I am about doing them. I realized that I was destroying myself and that I was a threat to the health and security of others and so gave up my bad habits. I stopped drinking and then stopped smoking. It so happened that the pain of withdrawal made me feel just as alive as did the drugs. This pain, no longer dull and nagging but bright and threatening, fanned my desire to break away from the demands that made me a substance abuser in the first place.

When I suffered from alcoholism I sought out other alcoholics and lived in an insular world that supported my disease. This is the wont of addicts—we search out people and places that make us feel normal, under-stood, even forgiven.

In the same way that I experienced my substance abuses many others of us suffer from another form of dependence: Americanism. This is not a physical drug but rather a system of ideas, and even ideals, that we crave, feel we need to make us whole and healthy. In order to imbibe this drug on a regular basis we have acquired great tolerance to lies, worldwide aggression, a completely integrated system of theft, and a monu-mental amount of pain and lifelong unhappiness.

Our drug is not a powder but a belief-system as absolute as any cult or mania.

We seek out other befuddled patriots and groups and live in an insular world that supports the notion of our righteousness even while our actions, beliefs, and attitudes are clear and present dangers to ourselves and every other living organism on the planet.

This *condition* seems to me to be the blockade keeping us from true political effectiveness and aware-ness. In order for us to come to a place where we can reap the benefits of our political responsibilities and human rights we must free ourselves from the emo-tional and economically based addictions that lay claim on almost every aspect of our lives.

And so I set out these twelve steps that if taken (to heart) might help us throw off the yoke of toil we strive under, opening a window onto a world that does not require us to be deaf to the cries of suffering, blind to crimes that are committed in our names, and silent about both these travesties.

Not all of these steps need to be taken in order. Some are *one-off* activities that can be achieved at almost any time along the way. But the first step must come where it is placed. Without this motion no other movement is possible.

# TWELVE STEPS
## TOWARD
## POLITICAL
## REVELATION

# ADMITTING THERE IS A PROBLEM AND DEFINING THAT PROBLEM

**T**his task is massive and ongoing, possibly never-ending. We face so many problems as denizens (not citizens) of the modern world that getting a handle on the definitions and interconnections of our afflictions and addictions might be the greatest co-nundrum we ever face.

From our bank accounts to our so-called health care system we are continually dealing with issues that defy our control. We live with machinery that chronically breaks down, debt that magically multiplies, poisons in the air and sea and earth, medical *care* that impoverishes us, and uncertain berths at jobs that slowly disintegrate our physical and mental well-being. We are fighting wars while feeling little patriotism and filling our prisons with millions of functional illiterates in a land that promises, no—legally requires—universal education.

We, most of us, live on the edge of poverty. Some own a home but can't afford food; others mortgage their property in order to eat, only to find that they may be evicted; many more move to the streets and are criminalized for the simple fact of their poverty. We drink to escape the thought of what we've become and are then arrested for our inebriation.

The great majority of Americans do not have enough in the richest country in the history of the world. Our labor, and our forebears' labor, has built a world that we don't own. Actually, this world is ours so long as we don't touch. It, that fabulously rich world, is our heritage but oddly not our inheritance. The only value we can lay claim to is contained in our decaying bodies. We can work until the strength and the will give out—and then we can die on the dole.

The dole: in a land where thousands of quite ordinary Joes are worth billions of dollars, each. The dole: in a land where the skim off the top of our labor made those unremarkable men and women so rich. The dole: in a land where our children go to war not out of choice but because they'd like to get an education and can't afford it on their own.

The funds for the dole are tapped whenever the government needs to finance a war or when those ordinary Joes have stolen too much and need to be bailed out. These funds are tapped when our armies are needed to ensure those Joes' foreign investments or to fight against the drugs that no tax can be levied against. This dole (our so-called social security and welfare fund) is shrinking while our elderly and impoverished population is growing.

I'm not just talking about the Social Security system here. There are thousands of private organizations that hand out blankets, hot meals, and chits to be used in homeless shelters. None of these charities (at least none that I know of ) are revolutionary. They don't organize the People to demand what is their rightful inheritance. They enable the poor to survive one day at a time until they fall by the wayside and someone else takes up their tin cups.

Between the government and private charities we have been lulled into accepting poverty, disease, homelessness, illiteracy, substance abuse, and the loss of our claim to dignity. We have been reduced to monadic particulates struggling to survive a game that was fixed before we were ever born.

So what we have are the fact of poverty and the prescribed moves we've been given to make that poverty somewhat palatable. We work and don't make enough to live on while residing next to and in the midst of opulence and plenty. We are allowed fast food, sex, cigarettes and alcohol, park benches, and mindless cinematic pabulum as legal, if partly proscribed, palliatives. We can also, with little resistance, take certain illegal drugs and involve ourselves in quasi-legal organizations and activities (such as gambling and prostitution) as long as we stay off the radar of those who are protecting the right of the Joes to accumulate their wealth in peace. We can be beautiful and lauded for that beauty. We can marry and set sail on the sludge of an endless sea that has slowly become a cesspool filled with the wastes of our aborted dreams. We can praise God as long as we don't take His word to heart.

The preceding paragraph is my admission, and partial definition, of the Problem. I see it as an economically based issue whereby the systems of wealth have subverted our political and human rights. We have been reduced from citizens to denizens and are allowed certain self-destructive behaviors in order to deal with the pain we have no choice but to endure.

This situation is far beyond serious but, still, not hopeless. We have the structure (if not the reality) of a democracy within our grasp. We have the potential to act against the tide of wealth stolen from our own pockets. And, most of all, we have the ability to clearly state the problems we face—and the most important step toward solving a problem is defining it.

[Before going on to Number Two in the Twelve Steps I want to say something about the dual nature of this book. On the one hand, I am completely committed to the content and arguments presented here. I believe that we have been turned inside out and against each other by the Joes (just another appellation for the mindless rich) and their herd dogs (lawyers and court-rooms, the army and police, and the schools that teach us to demand less of ourselves). We, the People, have been shunted out of the sphere of our rights and our inheritance. Recognizing our unconscious sorrow, the system of wealth has offered to sell us addictive prod-ucts, both physical and psychological, to console us on the long nights of isolation and, for the most part, un-recognized rage.

But, on the other hand, I see what I am presenting here as a kind of template that any nimble thinker can use to create another argument. One might think that the major problems we face are purely political, or that we need to begin with our morality and our faith. Even if I don't agree I won't argue against other interpretations of the issues we face. The only thing I need is for us to name and define the Problem(s). This has to be the first step. Without this knowledge the possibility of a road is lost.]

# THE IMPORTANCE OF LANGUAGE, OR LEARNING HOW TO SPEAK

In order to conceive of a problem on a social and/or political level we all need to have access to the same language; in other words, we need to achieve linguistic parity just to have the potential to take actions in concert.

When the first African slaves were brought to this continent, many and most were separated from others who spoke the same mother tongue. This was done to stymie the potential for rebellion. If you can't speak to your fellow slave, then you cannot fully identify with her. If you don't share words or identity with your workmates, your relationship to the master grows closer and the possibility of freedom fades—drastically. Without common language it is nearly impossible to plan an uprising or rebellion.

We, the People, are so separated: by dialects, religious teachings and iconography, education, age, and falsely perceived gender differences; by the opportunities given to some, by the Joes and their herd dogs, and taken from others; by laws and law enforcement, standardized testing, and a fabricated history that glorifies the few while silencing the many. We are turned against each other under the watch of officials elected by us but paid off by the Joes (the wealthy minority), by courts that have no commitment to the true balance of justice, by a system of profiling so sophisticated that most of us have no idea that potential allies are cut from the herd early so as to head off any possibility of resistance.

In order to heal our nation and move forward we have to start talking each other; we have to come out of our closets and dark alleys, we have to take off the blinders of semi-literacy and full-blown ignorance. This statement seems simple enough but is at the same time almost impossible to achieve: first, because we are convinced of the truths we know and have been taught (i.e., the pledge of allegiance, the arc of the land); and second, because even if we suspect that there is a truth beyond the language we speak, we do not have the ready tools (words) to access that truth.

So in order to begin talking about talking to each other we must first reevaluate the ways that we have been educated. I say this in the spirit that *you can't cry over spilt milk but you can clean up the mess*.

American education, especially public education, is sorely lacking. There's not enough money or time in school to adequately educate our children. Nor is there a commitment to, or even a clear broadly held picture of, what an educated citizen in the modern world should look like. Our teachers are overwhelmed and undereducated, while many parents are overworked and disengaged. Students are almost completely unaware of the empowerment that true education and literacy offer, and it seems that no one has figured out how to get through to the teachers, or the students and their parents.

Here in the land of plenty many working-class young people have no notion of how to live a healthy productive life. They eat fast food and seek after the distractions of sex, mass media, computer games, and worthless baubles. They live these lives simply because they don't know any better. It is not their imaginations that have failed them but their educations. They learn the little they know about life from the overstimulation provided by worldwide sports competitions, slack-jawed blockbuster film releases, ad men's impossible promises of youth and beauty, and the unattainable goals set by these public debacles.

The young people in America, whether they know it or not, are destined to carry the older generations on their backs. But they haven't been given tools to achieve this Herculean task. Without a proper education in the twenty-first century our descendents are bound to fail themselves and us.

To fulfill this aim—*a necessary education*—we need to concentrate on the positive space necessary to build the vital support structures of knowledge and communication. We know that our school system, teachers, and educational accessibility are lacking. But this, I believe, is due to lack of vision, not a lack of resources. If we cannot see the goal, how can we move toward it?

So what do we want to see in the education of our young people, and what does an educated young person look like in twenty-first-century America?

No one person can come up with the final answer to this question. There will be many different answers depending on the history, point of view, and aspirations of the school-system designers. What I propose here is a general outline that others can build upon, riff off of, and argue against.

Following is my suggestion for the universal education that all eighteen-year-old women and men of normal intelligence should have achieved at the end of a public school education.

1. They should be reading at a twelfth-grade level. This means that they should be able to read a challenging novel such as *Moby Dick* or a selection of *Leaves of Grass* and be able to understand the underlying themes, metaphors, and intentions of the work as well as the general meanings (i.e., story and plot).
2. They should be able to write a thousand-word essay explaining in cogent, systematic detail any feeling or piece of knowledge that they have.
3. Part and parcel of every American education should be the knowledge of history that includes *all* residents of, and immigrants to, these shores. Honest and unromanticized biographies of important historical figures, and as factual a

rendition as possible of the events of history, should be taught even though some acts may seem decidedly un-American.

But our graduating high school seniors shouldn't just have historical facts stored in their memories; they should also be able to question the genesis of any social situation, understanding that there are many sides to every story and that political history is often a misrepresentation of the real events.

4. All students, by the time they receive their diploma, should have a flexible grasp of the use of positive and negative space in the creation of at least one type of art. Whether this knowledge comes from an understanding of two-dimensional, sculptural, musical, or linguistic arts, they must understand what goes into creating the image, song, or story. With this knowledge (hopefully presented without the needless hierarchy of quality) our children will be able to cross the borders of imagination, allowing them openness to cross-cultural communication.

5. Scientific literacy is of prime importance in the development of the child and adolescent minds of America. A moderate knowledge of calculus, cellular biology, modern physics, Newtonian ver-

sus Einsteinian models of the universe, simple logic, and ecology is essential if our children are to be capable of reading a daily newspaper or blog, thereby connecting with the world around them. Our world works by technology and technique. If our youth do not know how it works, they will become the slaves of those who do.

6. Knowledge of their bodies has to be the one continuous subject throughout our young persons' early education. Rather than competition, their physical education classes should concentrate on how they can work together in coordinated efforts—how they can (must) depend on each others' strengths to achieve any goal.

    (I'm not completely negating competitive sports here. There is, of course, a place for them too. But it is a simple fact that most kids are not destined to *make the team*. This doesn't mean that their physical efforts cannot *make a difference*.)

7. Leadership training. As part of this element of an American education the population for most classes of children under the age of eighteen should be somewhere around a dozen students. Schools should be on the small side (three hundred or fewer students) and the highest expectations should be harbored for each member.

This said, I believe that a modified version of the Platonic ideal for government should be applied to every homeroom class. Student government should be both an elected body and a service duty that every student will be expected to participate in. What I mean by this is that certain key student-government positions should work on a rotating basis such that all students have an opportunity to experience the duty of decision-making for their classmates.

This experience will imprint upon our students the responsibility of political office and an understanding of governance and what is necessary for leadership.

8. Lastly, every student should be conversant in a foreign language. I, alas, speak only English. This lack makes me acutely aware of how isolated I am from a world that my monetary system at least partly dominates.

Once we understand what it is that our children should know when obtaining a required American education, we will know what is expected of ourselves.

But there is more, much more, to it.

In seeing what is possible in a pre-college education we can also begin to understand where even a good education fails. The acquisition of knowledge is a personal and therefore, in part, a unique experience. This individual aspect of the experience cannot be graded, nor should it be. A student who works only for a grade rather than for the joy and essential importance of knowledge will be limited by the expectations of others rather than exulting in self-growth.

Our best students, most of them, are limited by our own failed knowledge of how the world works and what is possible.

Passing a test in math does not make or define a mathematician. Reciting a passage of Aristotle does not make a philosopher. Of course students have to know certain facts and be able to work inside the logic of their chosen fields of study. But at the same time we, and they, must remember that Einstein had weaker math skills than most of the prominent physicists of his day. This lack did not keep him from being, arguably, the world's greatest physicist so far.

The question is, Does an education today allow every student to become the best he or she can be? The answer, I believe, is an unequivocal no. Teachers can fail. Parents can fail. On a broader plane, teachers and parents can be average or mediocre. But children are all and only the potentials for beauty, growth, and genius. They are not solitary receptacles of learning or cogs in the manipulation of knowledge. They are a whole nation waiting to blossom and come together to build upon each other in ways that we have never imagined.

It is only when we have mapped out the education we feel is necessary for our children as they head into this large and dangerous new century that we will know what it is we lack. A true knowledge and acceptance of one's deficiencies have a greater impact than any talent, test score, or excellent grade. Socrates realized that he was the smartest man in Athens because he knew his deficiencies and limitations, his ignorance.

We will increase our knowledge pool when we allow our children to rise above the little we know, our mundane understanding of possibility.

Our contribution to the new global dialogue will come through the mouths and ears of our children who—no longer competing against each other and us, nor hampered by the blinders of ignorance and functional illiteracy—will speak in a global language separate from the millennium we are leaving behind, a millennium that witnessed the Black Death, the Holocaust, slavery, and rampant unchecked Europeanized imperialism.

# STEP THREE

## TELLING
## THE TRUTH

**A**t the turn of the century I was asked to write a piece for presentation in London that told how I saw the coming of the new millennium. I decided to take on that job by looking at the past we seemed to want to escape so badly. A monograph came out of the talk called *Workin' on the Chain Gang: Throwing Off the Dead Hand of History*. I tried, in that first attempt at putting down my political impressions, to cover all the ills we were dragging along with us across a false notion of the border of time. I was satisfied with the book though it has its limitations and is already dated in many ways. I am happy to leave most of that monograph behind me. There is little in it that I want to repeat here—except for one idea.

This solitary notion is that it is the responsibility of each and every person in the nation to tell the truth at least once a day. This truth may be repeated but only if it falls upon ears that have not heard it from you before.

We live within an intricately woven fabric of lies. We lie about our children, our sexuality, our loves (and hates), our job histories, educations, experiences, our age. We lie to absolutely everyone, even, and most consistently, to ourselves.

We lie to our children, and our government lies to us. Advertisers have transformed the telling of lies to an art form. Historians fabricate with confidence and impunity. We tell lies and then, when we are found out, we lie about our deceits. *Yes, I did say that but I meant something quite different.* Our clothes lie about our bodies and our teeth lie about our smiles. We deny our actions even as we commit them.

The reasons for the war we are fighting in Iraq are based on lies. Our banks, our insurance and investment companies all lied about our money. Our religious and political leaders lie about their private lives with almost predictable regularity. Defendants in court prevaricate about their actions, and prosecutors twist the truth until it is worse than any falsehood.

Very few honestly believe what political candidates promise while running for office—we expect them to lie.

We expect to be lied to in almost every aspect of our lives; this fact is both a travesty and a tragedy because it opens the door for us to lie to ourselves. And if we accept that this notion of falsehood is at our very core, how can anyone trust us, how can we be trustworthy members of society? If we have accepted dishonesty into our hearts, have we not become the Prime Liars?

And let's not forget: How can a society be true to its destiny if even its execution of basic constitutional law is a perversion of itself?

We must pull away from the tide of lies and spread the truth (as well as we know it) to everyone who will listen. This action is essential if we are to begin to come to terms with each other. A common language arises not only from a proper education but also from pure expression and the desire not to hide.

*The truth will set you free.*

On the other hand, truth can be a hard taskmaster. Its telling may well put the speaker into jeopardy. If you speak out against a popular war or a belief about sexual acts that are unacceptable to the culture, if you no longer love your spouse or think that the leader of your group, organization, or office is behaving wrongly, you may very well be in for challenging times. This truth might set you free in an empty elevator shaft or send you careening off the side of a mountain.

But if there is no risk there is little possibility for gain.

Putting the antithesis and thesis together in this manner I believe that there might be a way for us to come to truth in our lives without destroying the little we have been given to survive on. That's why I suggest telling the truth only once every day. It could be a personal belief or conviction, an experience, an untold secret confided by a now departed relative, a desire, a medical condition, an addiction, even an admiration that you've felt but never expressed. Maybe you believe in the death penalty, or not; maybe you believe that God guides your hand or that your actions are governed by the economic infrastructure—it doesn't matter what you believe, your truth will certainly conflict with someone else's notion of reality. This is why we need to speak out. The truth we tell is not an end in itself. Speaking out will spark dialogue, and dialogue will rend the fabric of lies that cocoon us, the fallacies we live by but do not believe in.

Maybe you were the victim of a crime; maybe a perpetrator. Every day you might look out the window at a branch, noticing how it changes with the seasons and years. Maybe your eyesight is going but at the same time the acuity of your perceptions is increasing; maybe you have never experienced an orgasm. Truth is the grist for learning in adults and the adult world. If we all share what we know, what we believe, then we will change the world.

Lies promote darkness and injustice. This is why we live in a world that is so convoluted, why most of the only truth we hear is from TV sitcoms and cartoons, presented thus so that we can *laugh it off*.

The first handmaiden of this darkness is Silence; that which goes unsaid, that which is kept secret, and the real story that goes untold—all these are our enemies.

It is worthwhile for a moment to discuss the methodology of telling the truth each day. You might want to approach this exercise from different angles and trajectories.

Certainly you want to keep some kind of journal of your truths—a list in a password-protected file on your computer or a slip of paper that you carry around with you. There are a few reasons you might want to record these truths:

1.  You may think of something you believe at a time when it is inappropriate to voice it.
2.  You may need to examine a belief because it might be informed by some lie that you have swallowed whole.[*]
3.  The telling of a particular truth might cause undue pain to yourself or others.
4.  Writing in private is a good first step. Putting down your truth in words and looking at it is like a summoning; it calls forward something in you.

Of course, there is a certain danger in just writing down a truth. What if someone finds it? How will you feel having broached a subject that rattles you to your core? Feeling this threat is a marker for value in truth-telling.

On the other hand, keeping a journal of what you believe without bringing it into the world is akin to keeping silent. You have to speak out one day. You can start by talking to close friends and absolute strangers—

---

[*] Sometimes your feelings are not true. Hatred might really be jealousy or love. Fear of others might actually be fear of your own rage. Feelings of superiority might disguise an inferiority complex. It is worthwhile to live with your truth for a brief time before releasing it on the world.

friends because real friends will want to hear what you have to say and strangers because they have little power over your life. You can confide in a good friend about feelings that have festered in you but you have never voiced. And you can, for instance, tell a mechanic you never met before that you have always felt un-mechanical but believe that you really should know how the world works. The admission of ignorance is the first step toward understanding.

There is no truth too small.

The simple expectation that you have to say something once a day will have a great impact on your life. It will bring you into the world in a way that once seemed impossible. Every day will be an exploration into new territory. And, as the years pass, there is the possibility that a new person will emerge in you—a person you've always known about but have never met, a person you feel very comfortable with, a good friend you can trust to tell the truth.

As time goes by and you become comfortable with the truths in your life, you might want to start experimenting with how to express these newfound treasures in your heart and mind. Maybe you'll rent a billboard or take out an ad in the newspaper. Maybe you'll start a blog where you slowly expose the list that you've kept for so long in your wallet.

But even as I say this I am reminded that telling the truth is first and foremost an interpersonal enterprise. It is always best to meet with other people face to face and see how your reality reflects in their eyes.

The last element of this step is its antithesis—exploring the lies we tell every day. Each time you are about to lie, think about your action. Consider the message you are sending out into the world, the possible ramifications. Often you will go ahead with the fabrication, certain in your heart that what you are about to say will be for the best. But there will come an existential moment when you are aware of who you are and what you become when you spread your lies. This is a transitional moment, a potential epiphany. At this point you will begin to build the character and the conscience of a free citizen—a person who might even be able to rise above the rat maze of her or his life and see the true direction to follow.

# DEFINING
# THE CLASSES

I n the spirit of speaking of the truth: My awe of the power of the economic infrastructure causes me to believe that, as much as any other factor, our psyches are formed by our economic and technological interactions. We are, in part, defined by how we are organized inside, and against the underbelly of, the economic system.

The undereducated, impoverished worker who is destined to swing a sledgehammer, either on a construction site or on a chain gang, has a role and an identity that he must accept in order to fit in this world. In the same way, a Harvard business school graduate has a path set out for her. Most of us follow our paths with few questions. We even look forward, with dread or elation, to the milestones along the way.

The *fabric of lies* I referred to in the third step of this rehabilitation essay comes into play in the way in which classes are defined and how they see themselves.

The lower classes (i.e., sledgehammer swingers) are almost at the very bottom of the scale. They have the least influence and the lowest incomes. They live on the border of poverty and crime and are served last at the table. These are poor people. They do much of the most important labor in this world. They fill out the armed forces and police departments, accept the greatest levels of unemployment, do the heavy lifting, and keep the economy flowing in an upward trajectory. In almost all cases these people do not have enough money to afford comfortable lives. They go deeply into debt, which means that, as Tennessee Ernie Ford has told us, *they owe their souls to the company store*.

Some members of the lower (sometimes called working) classes become supervisors and managers, scraping out a little better living than those they lead. But these people also live near the edge of poverty, dreading the pink slip just as much as do all the others in the factories and warehouse-like offices.

Past the working class and working poor we have the beginnings of the middle classes: storekeepers and

CPAs, investment analysts and real estate investors, local bank managers and some artists, even some drug dealers, pimps, and illegal gamblers. The middle classes are the furnishing for the upper-middle classes and the wealthy; they are the flagstones and garden chairs, the one-night stands and yes-men. They, the middle classes, have a blue ticket that allows them to sit in the reserved seats at the back of the auditorium. This ticket also allows them to go back to the buffet table multiple (though not infinite) times. They are above the salt but nowhere near the head of the table. These people own the mortgage on an impressive home and have probably managed to finance a summer dwelling as well. They have all the accoutrements of wealth without much of a bank account to back it up.

After the middle and upper-middle classes we find the rich. These individuals own a great deal of the world we live in. They own the mineral rights on government lands, skyscrapers that house the corporations that govern most of our material interactions, vast tracts of empty land, and houses by the score. The rich don't have to work in the way that the classes below them do. Their money buys huge diamonds (but not diamond mines), extraordinary educations, and entrée into rooms that lesser class members don't even know exist.

The rich live by a different set of rules than most of the rest of us. The law usually treats them differently. The culture aggrandizes them simply because almost everyone else wants to have what they have.

Most people believe that the rich are the top of the food chain in modern capitalism. They have millions in the bank and can afford the best of everything.

This is almost the truth, but not quite.

There's an excellent TV cartoon show called *Futurama*. Its conceit is that a slacker from our age gets frozen and wakes up a thousand years in the future. The show also features a recurring character named The Honorable Judge Whitey. Once, when a case was brought before the judge, the accused was blamed for stealing some money. The judge was baffled for a moment and then said, *Ah, yes, money—that's what poor people use to get what they need to live*. I have never heard a better critique of the organization of modern capitalism. If you can count your money you might be rich, but your fortune doesn't hold a candle to the truly wealthy.

Wealthy individuals and corporations own the earth itself. Their property extends from horizon to horizon. You can't put a dollar value on their holdings because they fix the value of the dollar. The truly wealthy do not have a fixed worth. Their value is the blood in your veins and the invisible cell-phone waves rolling through the sky. They own, or control, the air we breathe and the water we drink. The wealthy own everything we need to survive.

This brings the definition of *class* full circle.

It is important for us to appreciate the structure of wealth in our world and to see ourselves, and others, in the places where we exist.

Some of the people reading this book belong to the upper classes. There might be one or two of the truly wealthy reading these words. But it's mostly working-class people who have this book in their hands—mostly because the vast majority of Americans are in the working class or lower.

In my opinion this truth should be self-evident. But the hidden truth is that many working-class people consider themselves middle class. This is a lie that has been foisted upon most Americans so that they will identify with the wealthy (masters) and not with the poor (wage slaves).

I'm middle class if I have a white collar and a bur-gundy tie. I'm middle class if I make over fifty thousand dollars a year. I'm middle class if my bank officer will loan me the money for a million-dollar house. I'm middle class if I read the *Wall Street Journal*. I'm middle class if all my friends say that's what they are.

What separates the working class from the middle class? A portfolio. If a middle-class person loses her job, her investment portfolio will pay her bills, her mortgage, her child's berth at Yale, her annual charities, and for her favorite restaurants and theater club season tickets for a year or a little more.

If a working-class person loses her job, her lifestyle will change drastically in two to four weeks. Debt will rise like a tsunami and all the frills that she bought on credit will wash away.

We have to be aware of these categories because that's the only way we can identify with each other and come together in political solidarity. The gates we run into are fencing us out, not protecting us. The politicians we vote for know our net worth better than we do. And net worth, the bottom line, is our most important political value.

Together *we* own the earth. Pretending that we are a part of the class above (or working toward being members of the class above) relinquishes our value to the powers that be.

By defining our class we can accurately see ourselves on the side where we exist without falling prey to the lies of bankers, politicians, and ad men. The wealthy control absolutely everything but We the People are the true custodians of Earth.

# LEGITIMIZING PSYCHOTHERAPY IN POLITICAL DEVELOPMENT

I have been in psychotherapy for well over twenty years. I started when I was in my early thirties and thoroughly lost. I had made it through college and worked my way up as a computer programmer but still I had that nagging feeling that I was in the slow lane in a perpetual interstate traffic jam.

I got a good recommendation for a well-known master-therapist and spent a week thinking of what I would say to him. After all, what excuse did I, a mere worker, have for sitting before such a distinguished and important man?

I knew that I was unhappy but there was no hook to hang my melancholy from, no phrase that accurately defined my malaise. I didn't think I was depressed, obsessive, or neurotic. I wasn't a substance abuser as I had given up tobacco and alcohol a decade before. I didn't know why I felt so lost. Maybe there was something very wrong with me. Maybe I was teetering on the verge of a nervous breakdown and didn't know it.

But *maybe* doesn't make a baby and *I don't know* doesn't tell you why you are here. So I sat me down and tried to come up with a picture that accurately defined who I was in the world, how I saw myself, and how I was slipping backward even while everyone else seemed to be moving ahead.

I came up with the following image:

*It feels as if everyone in the world begins at the same starting line. The starter pistol is discharged and we all move forward. Everyone else, it seems, is moving at a moderate pace of about ten miles a year while I am hurtling forward at a hundred miles a year and, at the same time, going backward at a ninety-nine-mile-a-year pace. And so at the end of every year I couldn't say that I was stalled, after all I'd made a mile's progress, but everyone else was ten times further along than was I. As the years pass I fall further and further behind—exhausted by the exertion of laboring almost twenty times harder than everyone else.*

I'm not sure how the head psychotherapist interpreted my explanation but he handed me over to one of his younger associates, with whom I have been working ever since.

This experience, this investigation of unconscious motivations for conscious acts, elated me. For the first time in my life, my life was the subject rather than how that life fit into the structures of a seemingly unreachable and capricious world.

Over time my relationship with the therapist has shifted. It started out with my trying to decipher emotional issues in an almost abstract vacuum. I saw myself and my world as I had been conditioned, and it took some time for me to understand about the untruths that I swallowed whole and swore by. But as the years have passed I have begun to use the time in therapy to figure out where I stand in my art, my personal relationships, my career, my political work, and in relation to the culture in general.

For me this experience has been invaluable.

Harking back to the step about truth-telling I am reminded that untruths come in all shapes and pretexts: We are lied to, we lie to ourselves, the truth is left unrevealed, we believe things that are obviously wrong, and, even worse, we want to believe what is obviously wrong. . . . This last form of lying is tricky and almost undetectable. I want to believe in my friends, workmates, the police, and our so-called leaders. When I am confused or in need I turn to these people for answers and help in figuring out my issues and problems.

Most of the time this is as it should be. My lawn is turning brown but Jack next door has the greenest grass I've ever seen. Of course I go over and ask him how he manages such an agricultural feat.

Someone breaks into my house and steals my TV and stereo equipment; the police are really the only option here.

I overlook the fact that Jack uses poisons to cultivate his grass and that the police spend their leisure hours profiling my friends and their children.

These barely hidden truths are the crumbling bedrock of our existence. The desire to ignore these truths is why most of us never try to climb out of the shambles of our lives.

What happens when you wake up one day and suspect that everything you do works against what you believe in—that the systems you turn to are actually predators in cops' clothing? What if you wonder whether you might serve your world and your moral beliefs better if you became a grassroots organizer on the other side of town, or a journalist/photographer in sub-Saharan Africa? Your father might ask how you will pay the rent. Your friends at the bank will not understand and tell you that it's just a phase. Your fiancé may ask, *How can we plan a future in the gated community when you work eighty hours a week for one-twenty-five an hour?* The profiling police department might even wonder if you have joined some kind of turban-wearing, bearded anti-American cell.

Very few people who have bought into the class system of the workaday world will support the changes in you. And even if some of your friends and acquaintances do seem to understand, this understanding will come on their own terms with their own agendas (consciously or unconsciously) attached. The director of the grassroots organization will support your impulse whether or not the move is good for you. The group looking for photographers may not warn you that you might be putting your life in jeopardy in a hostile environment. Your own mother may love you and support you but still not understand a word you're saying; you may not understand yourself.

These problems arise because unexamined subjectivity rules the format of the vast majority of human actions and interactions. We are conditioned to have expectations in our jobs, our relationships, our aesthetics, even in death. We most often work against ourselves and try to keep each other in line doing the same thing. We do this to have a sense of security in our lives. We expect conformity so that we don't have to think about what we're doing and what our neighbors are doing behind closed doors.

Psychotherapy, for all its potential value, has many of the same problems. The use of prescription mood-altering drugs, anesthetizing exercises, and good old-fashioned phrases like *You're as normal as I am* often roll off the psychotherapist's desk and out of his mouth. Most people seek out therapy so that they might fit better in a bad marriage, under a tyrannical boss, in a world where their own government declares war on the poor and weak and innocent. They ask, *How can I live with this pain and this guilt?* But the real question that should be asked is *How can I live?*

There are some therapists out there who try to attain a level of *objectivity*. Just the attempt to achieve impartiality is what we need more than anything to make decisions in a world where we are ripped off, bamboozled, and then blamed for our own condition.

> PATIENT: *Am I wrong to be angry that I work sixty hours a week and still can't afford to send both of my children to the colleges they want to go to?*
> THERAPIST: *What do you think?*

I know this appears to be a simple counter-interrogative but it is really a revolutionary exchange. The therapist is not making a moral judgment on the patient, she is not trying to say that he should grin and bear it. If the questioner (patient) says that he feels guilty or that he is angry, or has any other response, the dialogue will go from there. The purpose is to examine the problem in relation to how you feel, to decipher the conundrum that flummoxes you. You do not arrive at a *you-should* kind of answer but at *you-are* or *you-want*. This is as close to objectivity as we're ever going to get. No one is ever truly objective but that really isn't necessary—all you have to do is try to allow the emotions to arise from the person experiencing them. In this atmosphere the patient has the potential to find out what he really feels and what he really wants. Between feeling and want is the closest we'll ever come to understanding who we are and where we might go.

The road to revolution cannot be traveled alone. The movement will have its leaders and followers, its theorists and soldiers, its full adherents and its less committed—but all of these will have to work together in order to bring us out of the malaise and into something like a concrete idea. And objectivity is the unreachable standard that we must strive for. In an off-quote from the poet: *What is is, is the only way I can conceive of change.*

The gesture toward objectivity (*is*), therapy (*is*), and unity (*is*) comes together in a way that is unique in our political history. In that trinity we might find some answers that go beyond patriotism toward a kind of necessary humanism.

One final note on the primary assumption of this step:

I refer to the person who goes to the therapist as a *patient*. There is serious intention behind this word. We, most of us in modern-day America, are sick. We suffer deep emotional displacement from the lies we are told and the subsequent lies we tell ourselves. I'm fine, doing well. I'm safe. I'm part of a healthy, democratic polity. I am helping my children to become whole, healthy individuals.

None, or at least little of this, is true. Tens of thousands of our children die in foreign wars and prisons, from drug addiction and substance abuse. The great majority of our poor are children and their mothers. The elderly are systematically stripped of their wealth and dignity. Life itself is defined by alienated labor for the vast majority of our people, and truth is a rarer commodity than moon rocks.

Make no mistake—we are a society of ailing denizens. We need treatment for our infected souls.

# EVERY DAY

The most important lesson I've learned as a writer is that practice of the art is something I must exercise every day. The reason for this constant training is that any idea worth discovering is bigger than my head. The twists and turns, story and plot, characters and character development of a novel cannot be held in a single thought or even in a train of thought. This novel takes up a lot of space and needs room to breathe and evolve.

Another way to look at the novel, rather than by its girth, is its depth. Most of the ideas of a novel exist beneath the waves of consciousness, deep in the pre- and unconscious folds of our experience (which, in its totality, is also larger than the head—or conscious mind). Every time we begin writing, the door to this deep well of feeling and knowledge opens a crack. We peer through this tiny aperture and get down some words. For the rest of the day we might be completely oblivious to what we wrote that morning but the ideas are still there. Like invisible hummingbirds in a cave, the thoughts broached in that morning session send out subliminal vibrations that travel in the darkness hitting upon hitherto unguessed at notions and ideas that, in turn, shudder in sympathy. . . .

Now we are at a crossroads. When we wake up the next morning that door of perception is still ajar, the hummingbirds are still aloft, and the ideas, once in darkness, are now faintly illuminated by what has gone on the day before. If we sit down at our desk and start writing again, these new ideas, one way or another, will work their way into the writing. But if we don't sit down and take advantage of what we discovered— seemingly by chance—the door will close and we will be, once again, locked out of our own ideas.

The best way, sometimes the only way, to succeed at writing a novel (or essay) is to write every day, seven days a week, three hundred sixty-five days a year. You don't have to write for a long time, just long enough to peek into the darkness and listen for that sympathetic humming just beyond the range of what you can see and know for certain.

This exercise is not only of value to the artist. Returning every day to the subject of your life is the most important implement in the toolbox of the worker who wants to short-circuit the oppressive nature of the modern world. The economic, political, and governmental systems of the world work every hour of every day. These systems strive to maintain the definition and the direction of your world. They define the value of your labor and the quality of your education, the candidates for your votes and the timetable by which your streets are fixed. The powers that be are working all the time to organize your labor against your goals. And if you don't spend at least a couple of hours *every day* working to articulate and effect your desires, you will be defeated by the system's daily counter-attempt to destroy your individuality.

I don't want to sound paranoid in saying that it is the intent of the structures of the modern world to quash our distinctiveness, but I believe that this is an obvious fact. We are taught to *fit in* from the earliest stages in our schools, churches, workplaces, and just walking down the street. Our questions, our instincts, our desires to live lives that are not defined by these institutions are pushed down and ultimately disabled.

It is the corporation's job to make the greatest profit off of your labor, not to make sure you have medical care, adequate retirement, or deep joy and satisfaction in your everyday experience of life. Sometimes a corporation might do something positive for you, but this is because of a conflict with a separate institution like a union or the federal government. Some more *enlightened* conglomerates realize that a happy worker might, for a time, produce more profit if given a chance at happiness. But even this chance will be taken away if it subsequently loses its profitability.

I'm not talking about good and evil here. I'm mapping out systems and the ways in which those systems work against the Free Will of their students and employees, soldiers and citizens (denizens). A CEO—Joe #25,362—might decide that he loves his workers and wants to make sure that they all get childcare. But that extra twenty-five hundred dollars per worker per year will show up on the corporate bottom line and the business will falter in its competition with similar firms; the CEO will be replaced by Joe #25,363 or the company will go out of business; either way, the chance for a corporate nursery will be lost.

The economic system* works like the internal systems of any living body: Needs are encountered and needs are met. It's just that simple. Resources are devoured and wastes are removed. The corporation is the Great Shadow Joe that hovers above our lives. It doesn't, it can't care about us on human terms because it is not human. It is a virtual beast, a humungous parasite that feeds off of our labor and off of the natural resources that by rights belong to us. It uses our technology, our language, our own image to manipulate and mime us but it can never empathize with flesh and blood, dreams and terrors.

This system is both intelligent and mindless. It works in symbiosis with our needs but it is not us. The Great Shadow Joe moves like a shibboleth through our lives, our bodies, our friends and foes, children and lovers. It creates us, or re-creates us, in its own image, leaving us with the notion that we ourselves decided to buy that red truck or kill that hill farmer seven thousand miles away.

Shadow Joe never gets tired because he is a virtual entity using our reorganized labor for his energy. Wake up at night and Shadow Joe will be waiting for you on

---

* Which in most respects is the template for our social, government, and military systems.

the TV. Walk down the street and he will call to you from billboards and display windows. Walk the fields of your ancient homeland and he might rain billets or daisy-cutters down upon you. He is nearly unrecognizable (not unlike the novel that lives in each and every one of us) and we aren't looking for him—at best we only suspect his existence.

The reason Shadow Joe isn't on everyone's lips is that he (like the novel) resides inside our minds. He is bigger than anything a normal human can conceive of in a single thought—or train of thoughts. He is everywhere in our culture and economy like a bad case of trichinosis.

The only way to remove this systemic infection is to work at it slowly and methodically—every day.

Every day you have to sit with yourself and try to figure out what is right and what is wrong in your life. You need to write these ideas down, consider them, edit them, then rewrite them. The world will not change without you changing. You cannot change without working every day to discover the secrets, and lies, hidden inside your Shadow Joe–fabricated mind.

The purpose of your life is to discover the great edifice of possibility and hope hidden in your heart. It is a treasure that has been buried there and then laid claim to by Shadow Joe.

Set aside ninety minutes a day to sit down to a journal where you write about what you think might be going on in the world around you, what you are worth, and where you would go if the barriers of everyday life were lifted.* From these down-to-earth questions you will have built a firmament that will, necessarily, militate against the Joes and their God (the Great Shadow Joe). Your hard work, strength, and youth have been used to build the power of the Joes. Once you take these fuels away, their system will dim and your potential will grow.

But, most importantly, you will have to go through this exercise every day. In doing this you will begin to understand that many of your thoughts and aspirations don't come from you. Your true desires have been rerouted and tied off. Many of your ideas today will seem simplistic, or even wrong, tomorrow. This is the process of creativity at work. You try one thing and realize that it's wrong but you learn from the mistake and try something else. Months after writing a line you come back to it and realize that there is a whole paragraph behind it—a paragraph that says something altogether different.

---

* This will, in part, also be your truth journal.

If you work every day at trying to understand the world in which you live, the growth you experience will be exponential. Shadow Joe is large but he is not truly great. We are the building blocks of his systematic repression of our lives and our needs. When we push back with regularity and burgeoning comprehension, he must ultimately transform into something closer to his aggregate parts.

One thing to remember here is that the system thrives when its parts are all the same and therefore replaceable. The ideas that grow from your every day exercise need not equal what others have found in their self-interrogations. We must be able to communicate with each other but we don't have to share the same ideas. We need to come to terms but not to fit into molds that provide false security.

# STEP SEVEN

## MAKING
## DEMOCRACY

**A**merica is an oligarchy in democratic clothing. Our body politic is amorphous and intangible and therefore our actions cannot match our intentions; this disconnect is due to the fact that our political leaders are vetted by special-interest corporations that say they are political parties (i.e., Democrats and Republicans). These special-interest corporations dominate all three of the major platforms of federal representation (also state and local governments); they are owned by clients (the Joes) who pay for services rendered. They divide us by taking specific differences and unfounded fears and using these to drive wedges between the working-class denizens who should see themselves as one people rather than as innumerable castrated tribes.

People often tell me that America is a democracy because people have the right to vote. I reply that people voted in the old USSR too—but so what? If we are unable to come together in our voting, if we are ruled out of real choice by so-called party politics, then how can we say that we're living in a democracy? If millions of dollars have more power to influence than the truth does, then how can we honestly say that we have a working democracy?

Justice in America is more a commodity than it is anything else. The rich have better lawyers at their side and people who understand their inner turmoils sitting upon the bench; they have prosecutors who can be overruled by backroom politics and enough dollars to pay for special treatment if they happen to receive a lesser sentence.

And if there is no balance in justice, how can there be democracy? If we, in our hearts, accept the disparity of our own system, then we abrogate our rights as citizens. But don't get me wrong—this is not a condemnation of the will of the American people. The only mistake we have made is that we believe that the system is insurmountable and that wealth somehow has to have its privileges because there is an indefinable and inescapable affinity between capitalism and democracy.

In truth, capitalism is closer to totalitarianism and fascism than it is to the democratic process; that's why unions appeared and why Congress once led a campaign against monopolies and cartels. Democracy has nothing to do with the decision-making process in the organization of capital. The wealthy would like us to think that it does. That's why they build monuments to themselves, name foundations after their families rather than after the people they set out to *help*. The only affinity that the wealthy have with democracy is their money and their control of the media. They tell us the news, dress up the candidate, set the value of our dollars and our labor until the poorest among us join the army to slaughter other poor people in the name of freedom while the wealthy are safe and richer each day.

But, like I said, this is not condemnation of the American people. The economic system has so deeply insinuated itself into our everyday lives that it seems impossible to dislodge. Billionaires and their millionaire-minions control the majority of newspapers, TV shows, movies, and magazines, Congress, the army, the police, and even the schools and schoolbooks to promulgate their message until there seems to not even be a toehold that we can manage in order to resist the overwhelming pressures brought to bear on us.

The earth is flat, just look at my carpenter's level.

But all is not lost.

Jacques Ellul and Lewis Mumford tell us that not only technology but also technique (the way in which labor is executed and imagined) have toppled more civilizations than any creed or revolutionary outcry. A simple technological invention like a superior screw can so alter the economics of a culture that the old ways are forced to fall by the side of the road, making way for new organizations, politics, and governments.

It is my fervent belief that the cigar-smoking backroom politicians of the latter half of the twentieth century are about to meet their fatal screw.

The problem with true democracy in America is that our nation is far too large for the plethora of political interests to organize themselves against the fairly small range of interests pursued by big business. On one side you have a group of wealthy individuals, families, and corporations that have the simple goal of wanting control of the means and the mode of production. They achieve these ends by bringing about lower salaries, buying up cheap mineral rights, breaking unions, out-sourcing labor, and convincing us to give them a healthy bailout if these machinations go awry. On the other side you have the abortionists and anti-abortionists, separatists and integrationists, universal marriage con-stituents and those who believe that gay marriage is somehow immoral, PETA adherents and the right-to-bear-arms hunting enthusiasts. There are ten thou-sand other interest groups all of whom can find as many iterations of their opposites in the spectrum of our so-called democracy.

How can we, the People, stand against the highly organized and simplistic needs of the Joes when we are so separated and fragmented by ten thousand thou-sand conflicts?

The answer is (at least from my point of view) to use the Internet (that new screw) and an equation that will allow us to stop working against each other and begin to work together on the topics where we agree.

What I propose is a website called The Democracy Initiative. On this website each of us can identify our ten most pressing political interests in order of importance—for example, (1) the right to bear arms, (2) equal rights for women, (3) universal marriage rights. Once we've identified our convictions in a national (and international) database we can find those others who are of a similar state of intention *without* having to know about their commitments that are antithetical to ours. As the song says, *accentuate the positive.* This will allow the black nationalist and white supremacist to vote together for the rights of poor children to have medical care; the anti-abortionist and the pro-choice advocate to unite against the war.

We have more in common than we are against each other. It is only the big dollars of big business that separate us. But the technology and potential technique of the Internet open a door for us to unite outside of the edicts and directions of the so-called political parties, the Joes, and the Great Shadow Joe.

The new technology can bring down the walls of the oligarchs; it can allow us to unite and change politics from an adversarial stance to one of unity.

This is my ardent desire—to allow the individuals of our virtual democracy to come together on their own terms, not on the made-up issues of the wealthy who only wish to divide the lower classes and therefore shore up their position while keeping us groveling for crumbs.

And so, even if my articulation here is not at the moment technically possible, there is at least a strategy for an attempt at building an underground system of democracy against the surface lies of the special-interest parties.

And let me underscore the core belief of this Democracy Initiative: *Objectivity*. This is not a left or right question. Democracy is for all of us; for the voter, the child, the lonely prisoner, and those who live here without the benefit of citizenship; it is for black and white, young and old, educated and uneducated, lovers and haters. We must support a system based on our participation no matter where that participation leads.

# STEP EIGHT

## ATTEMPTING TO UNDERSTAND THE MIND IN RELATION TO THE ECONOMIC INFRASTRUCTURE

The late nineteenth and the twentieth centuries could be looked at as the testing grounds for what I call the *School of Suspicion*. This approach to discipline is the study of a world, or a system of worlds, that cannot be seen by the naked eye, understood by the conscious mind, or brought into focus by the cause-and-effect lenses of animal awareness. The *School of Suspicion* comes out of Einstein's negation of Newton, Freud's articulation of a completely unconscious mind that guides conscious human actions,

Darwin's notion that life is never an endpoint but always in the midst of bubbling biological change, and, of course, Marx's position that human organization is based not upon gods or the rights of kings but upon the complex dialectics put into play by the economic infrastructure. Marx tells us that we are slaves to this system of economics—that our minds and social organizations are dictated by the means and the mode of production.

One does not have to agree completely with Karl to accept the fact that the way we do business affects the way we live life in forms that are incomprehensible to the logical and objective mind.

Women are being raped by the tens of thousands in the Congo, hundreds of thousands of times, at least in part because of the worldwide need for the chemical—Coltan—that is used to make cell phones. The coveting of oil under the ground causes devastation in the towns and villages above. The concentration of wealth creates poverty; charity then continues rather than alleviating the disparity. Crazily, race is created by racism, which itself was brought into being by imperialism, under the rules of colonization and now under the new guise of globalization. Criminals are created by the division of labor and the kinds of personalities needed to satisfy production. Alcoholism, drug addiction, and neuroses to a great degree are reactions to this organization of labor and the products it creates. Entire groups of indigenous peoples live on land they do not control. The atmosphere itself is a casualty of unnecessary waste and meaningless production.

Everything happens for a reason (maybe) but these reasons are not immediately knowable. How can I and my ancestors have built this great wealthy nation but still be poor? Why are our most revered institutions seemingly blind to the blights of obesity, illiteracy, disease, gangs, bloated prisons rolls, and common feelings of hopelessness and impotence?

Does someone up there hate us?

No.

The economic infrastructure calls for these situations, afflictions, and cyclic pain. The way we are organized to live and work, eat, and resist the ravages of nature, makes us into economic mutants that have no notion of the origins of our self-mutilations.

This step begins with the word *understanding*. It goes without saying that we have to understand the nature of our oppression before we can counter it, but in this case I'm using the word in its most active form. I believe that we need to understand the economic in-frastructure in the same way a psychotherapist believes that we need to comprehend unconscious motivations in our psyches.

Don't get me wrong here: I am not a proponent of psychoanalysis-proper, nor am I a Marxist. But I do believe that the *School of Suspicion* has opened doors to motivation in our hearts, lives, and the physical world—doors that we cannot ignore. How people live their lives originates in places that they have never been taught to question.

What I am proposing is a kind of Marxian Psy-choanalysis that has as its goal the understanding of how our organization of labor and wealth creates the situations of our everyday lives and the bugaboos in our minds.

Almost everybody works for a living. We work hard, most of us. From the CPA to the corner heroin dealer, we all work. And you can't work unless there's a job to do. That's why there are no blacksmiths today: No one needs a blacksmith and so no one will pay for that job. But people do need accountants and drugs and women raped to keep them from getting in the way of the system of profit; we need mercenaries to kill Iraqis and a president to toe the line; we need scientists and street sweepers, prostitutes and priests. Our needs create our world and, in turn, the world we create re-forms our needs. This wobbly spiral of human life and economy, which has many elements in common with the theory of evolution, is what we have to question if we are to understand and take control of our (human) destiny.

Once we accept the fact that everything happens for a reason (and that that reason is often based on production, labor, and need) we can begin to decipher the problems we have. Once we have even the dimmest notion of the purpose of an action, no matter how heinous or self-destructive, we will find ourselves on the road to recovery.

Consider the blue-collar worker who has received inferior schooling that has prepared him for only low-level labor and income. It is easy to understand why this worker either sells or uses drugs in order to cope with the oppressive configuration of his life. With just this small bit of knowledge we understand that this worker's suffering must be alleviated if we wish to change the situation. Law, morality, feelings of intellectual superiority fly out the window when we look at social situations through the lens of labor, production, and survival.

Sometimes a woman just needs a drink: Either give her the drink (soma) or assuage the need.

We need to put our culture on the analyst's couch if we want to understand our minds in this world. Mother-love is potent but so are unemployment and prison. Unconscious drives motivate everyone but so do the thrumming needs of the economic infrastructure. Evolution makes and remakes us with every generation (indeed with every birth) but a revolution festers in the cracks of the *School of Suspicion* and we are on the verge of making the leap from blindness to blinding light.

I am progressive politically but this particular step is not necessarily progressive. Once you understand the underlying economic reasons for a social woe you might not take an action to relieve that problem. I can only hope that, once people see that the forces that drive our enemies also drive us, they will want to sit down and reorganize the systems that have so warped our world.

# DISCONTINUING THE PRACTICE OF LIVING IN THE PAST

The older we get the more we live in the past. Memories and beliefs blend with contemporary images beheld by our old eyes and we begin to see things that aren't quite there. If you learned survival from the Depression or a war, if you came to understand others through an old manifestation of racism or sexism, if you came to know the world through paper and ink rather than screens and keyboards, you may have a vision of the world that has ever-lessening relevance. But regardless of the waning significance of your knowledge and awareness you are regarded, and regard yourself, as well-educated, knowledgeable, and maybe even influential; maybe you are—influential—but that doesn't make you right; you might very well be making decisions based on experiences, and supposed truths, that no longer govern the world we live in.

The reason you seem so smart and current is not because you live in this world today but because you have agglomerated wealth and mastered a backward-looking but dominant system of articulation and communication.

In truth, in many ways, the younger generations know this world better than their elders simply because the world as it is is *all* they know. From computer systems to the distribution of wealth, young people have important contributions to make to the general dialogue about the way things actually are and, therefore, how change might be effected.

We cannot blame the youth for the TV shows, movies, ads, and campaigns that rob them of their wealth and (seemingly) their sanity. The term *bling* was co-opted by Madison Avenue and made into a billion-dollar business that the youth feed into but do not, in any meaningful way, profit by. Our culture, economy, and any hope for a future lie heavily on the backs of our youth—and they know it. They rhyme about it and live out the frustrations in the streets and in their veins. They know many things but we also robbed them, most importantly, of a proper education that might enable them to speak to us about their world in our nomenclature.

The innocent future of the world belongs to the young while the past is our crime. My generation—the generation that, for the most part, sat by witnessing the holocaust of Cambodia, Vietnam, Chile, and elsewhere—now has rising ire against inner-city gangbangers and drug dealers. Can't we see these actions as attempts for (a small portion of) our youth to bring organization and a conception of justice into their lives? Can't we see that we forced this world into existence even as we now abandon it for the sweet dreams of a past that may have never been?

From our strongholds, our belief in a world that has long-since passed its zenith, we control and then castigate the young as they suffer for our mistakes. Do we honestly believe that the young have refused to take up the reins, to obtain a useful education, to face adulthood while at the same time living within a worldwide system of consumerist infantilization? After all . . .

who makes the video games and *bling*, the fancy shoes and TV *reality* shows? The young people don't own or control this world; they merely finance it with their sparse dollars, their blood and souls.

What am I trying to get at in this diatribe? It's simple: We (the supposed elders) have to begin to create a collaborative relationship between ourselves and the youth of America and the world. We have to realize that we can't just ask inner-city youth to give up their gangs and music while we go banging away at foreign nations with abandon and even celebratory élan. We can't complain about the untrustworthiness of our young when our own bankers, congressmen, insurance companies, and financial advisors rob us blind and then ask to be bailed out, forgiven, and reelected. We have to sit at the table with the youth of our nation and change and grow as much as we are asking them to change and grow. Through this dialogue we have to learn from them as we expect them to learn from us. We have to give up some control, some money, and most of our connection to a dissipating image of the past.

The young people are the only ones who can take care of this world. . . . We need to make an absolute commitment to them.

The process of this step is to begin questioning our beliefs. For instance:

Recently a conservative candidate for president sang a rousing chorus of *bomb, bomb, bomb . . . bomb, bomb Iran*, a takeoff on a pop song of the middle '60s. This bastardization of a forty-year-old song made clear my fear that so many people in power live, and thrive, in the past.

Maybe in the '50s and '60s brute force was a workable method of curtailing nuclear proliferation; maybe we could attain our ends by flexing our muscles in those long-ago days. Looking at this stance from today's standpoint we might have been wrong even then, but today there is no question that our hegemony over weapons of mass destruction is over. Within a decade countries like Togo and Luxembourg will have the wherewithal to produce and deliver these terrible products.

If we follow these archaic templates of balance, the world will suffer from it. We need diplomacy and communication to stem the potential for violence on a grand scale. Young people are at the forefront of communication if only because they constantly create one of the most universal languages—popular music. We need to bring them into our meetings and discuss with them, as equals, the problems we all face in this twenty-first-century village of ours.

The older generation's decisions, to a great degree, are based on misplaced certainty and fear whereas the youth have optimism and a much healthier learning curve than our aging brains can muster. We must cut away that which is no longer useful in our stores of memory and bring what's left, our valid experience, to our young people. Together we have a chance of creating international parity and a country where brothers and sisters come in all ages, sexes, races, and creeds.

# UNDERSTANDING COST

Cost. The Great Shadow Joe and his acolytes, the Joes, grasp this term with uncanny acuity. They know what everything costs down to the micro-mil: planks of wood, fish off the coast of Brazil still swimming and dreaming of the filtered sun, unending acres of fallow earth in southern Wyoming, the labor in your hands and in your aging brain. They know how much it costs to get a left-handed person to buy a product in a market versus the cost of snagging a right-hander. They understand the way to bring you to life in steps from sexual arousal, to desire for comfort, to the cash register—all while you're talking to your mother on a cell phone about Christmas dinner.

Having the knowledge of what things cost provides almost absolute power in the modern world. If you know what something costs then you have at least the potential to control that thing. There are people in Washington and on Wall Street who can tell you how much it will cost to make a young woman a doctor or to maintain a young man's lifelong journey through the prison system once he has slipped (or has been pushed) into the gangs.

This might be the most important and complex step in the recovery program of the Oppressed Denizen of the modern world—this because Cost is an intricate process that appears to be simple. It (Cost) started out purely and innocently as a human bartering system but through the centuries it has been taken over by the virtual system of the Great Shadow Joe. Capitalism (GS Joe's other name) has altered Cost and value to fit its needs and predilections.

There was a time that an old woman sitting in front of her semi-rural home in Oregon could tell you what an apple in her barrel cost. No more. Now Best-Fruits-Imaginable, an agribusiness cartel officed in Cincinnati but incorporated in São Paulo, Brazil, can undersell that grandmother and tell her, by the greatest of all communicators (The Market), what the true and transitory worth of the product of her family's age-old orchard actually is.

"But, Miss Rogers," the potential buyer says, "I can buy a whole bag of apples like these at the supermarket for the price you're charging for one."

Cost.

As everyday citizens in the world who know our alphabet and our numbers, we believe that we understand Cost. The price tag says *apples $3.25 a bag*. I can read. I can comparison-shop in the newspapers. I can call Betty and ask her how much she's paying across town. I don't need a weatherman to know which way the wind blows.

Au contraire.

The price tag has nothing to do with Cost. The price tag is what you pay—right now. But every dollar you spend is only a down-payment on a bill that will follow you for the rest of your life. Once Best-Fruits-Imaginable buys 87.09 percent of the mom and pop orchards in the Northwest, apples might well become a rarity and their Cost will reflect their availability. The apples you bought five years ago at a discount will now eat into your paycheck as you bite into them. These are the wages of Cost.

And it goes further than that. What does a high-fat, fast-food, antibiotic-treated, whole herd of cattle in a single burger cost? It's probably cheaper than you can make at home; but what about the addictions that you and your children develop to fast foods? What about the clogged veins, obesity, diabetes, heart disease, colon problems, and a host of other maladies? What do they cost?

What does vengeance cost? The starving children in Afghanistan and the shell-shocked citizens of Iraq may not be on the radar of most Americans, but what about our own disabled and traumatized soldiers who went to War because they couldn't afford the Cost of living as young working-class citizens of this country. Who pays? Who profits? Who makes the decision, and who is told what they will pay regardless of what they want, what they earn, and what they're worth?

Using War as an example of Cost we can begin to see the crystal-like complexities of Cost connected to any action we take or exchange we make in the Modern World.

Buy an apple from the supermarket and drive Miss Rogers out of business.

Join the army because you can't get an education and kill innocents, all the while addling your own mind.

Buy a house and go bankrupt.

Cast a vote the way some people buy lottery tickets.

Almost every action we take has an effect that we did not intend, an effect that Costs us more than it provides for our comfort and ease, health and well-being.

Whatever something Costs in the Great Shadow Joe's domain—it is worth less. This is the rub. This is the instant when we give up our value to the greater system. And this gift is not to an entity that cares about us or our well-being. Above our heads, in the ether of capitalism, there is a continual war being waged between virtual corporate gods—Best-Fruits-Imaginable versus Mantan Applesauce, Tolmec Investments versus Less Bank, General Hospital versus If You're Lucky Health Insurance. These warrior gods are animated and empowered by our labor, our dollars. As their battles intensify we are drained of more and more of our resources. As we get weaker they get stronger. Costs rise at the supermarket and in the taxes and even in our veins. We pay out of our pockets, we pay in secret charges, we pay in outrageous interest rates, and we pay just by working and being undervalued by the servants of the virtual war being fought in the heavens of our own imaginations.

Okay. That's the uppermost surface of the problem. We work and then receive less than the value of our labor; we pay more than what we buy is worth. The systems that these exchanges are based on are decided by virtual entities (i.e., corporations) that are alien to our biologies and therefore have no ability to identify or empathize with our problems. It *seems* as if human beings govern these interchanges but, in truth, this is not so. Individuals can prosper from the systems of Cost only as long as they go along with the rules. No one who breaks the rules may stay in control.

How do we, Everyday Denizens, counteract this tautological economic trap?

To begin with, we have to come to some kind of understanding of worth versus Cost. What am I worth? What am I paid? What is the worth of the things I buy versus the price I buy them for? Once we begin to have a notion of the answers to these questions we can begin to organize ourselves against the Great Shadow Joe and his invisible machinations.

I am about to embark on some very murky waters here because I am not an economist and so don't have the training to present arguments in those terms. But I do have some common sense and an appreciation for what is necessary to enter a conflict between any two entities.

In order for someone to challenge me, my Opponent, if he has any hope of winning, must bring at least equal strength into the conflict. This strength may be defined in different ways: It might be skill versus brute power, reach versus close-to-the-ground weight, determination versus self-confidence, or just the power of one opponent to *psyche-out* the other. These rivals will be more or less evenly matched (because the fight is the thing: the debacle that is our *open* market).

Our Opponents, the Joes, have an in with the promoter (the Great Shadow Joe) and have gone to great lengths to fix the fight in their favor. They have defined everything from the size of the ring, to the referee, to the judges. They own the experts who have written how we (the consumers) are the underdog. They have even created advertisements that show every blow we have ever received while, alternately, showing every punch that our Opponents have delivered. They have filled the auditorium with their supporters gratis while charging our followers a thousand dollars a seat.

Conversely, they have hinted, here and there, that their favorite might have an injury, that the underdog has a slugger's chance, that this is a fair fight and any-one can win.

We are dreading defeat but given hope at the same time. In this way we keep on fighting but without much heart.

The boxing metaphor, I believe, works. It leaves us with the suspicion that there might be other ways to win this fight—a fight whose very nature is the state of our economy. There are two major ways that we can begin to plan for victory: by realizing (1) that the Joe in the other corner is our equal and (2) that we don't have to fight the way he expects.

To speak to the first part of the *plan for victory* I believe that we should use a rule of thumb to gauge what is happening to us in the so-called open market: That is, for every dollar we make, the Joes take a dollar for themselves (maybe a few mils more) and for every dollar we spend we get fifty cents or a little less in value. And, even though these two claims have to be true in order for the Joes to challenge us, the wealth is all cre-ated by us. The wealth is ours and we have to begin taking it back. We have to begin to make a ceiling for profit on necessities just like there is a floor for wages. Food, for instance, should not exceed a 10 percent profit margin; neither should primary-home real estate. Economic corruption by elected officials has to come with heavy penalties, and citizen review boards need to be set up to oversee the uses and abuses of our various branches of government and bureaucracy. All primary service providers (banks, hospitals, insurance companies, supermarkets, and natural-resource providers) must be held to this standard. You can profit, but only by a strictly maintained margin. I don't care about bling. If a jewelry store wants to charge $100,000 for a silver hoop—that's fine with me. But apples and pears, work shoes, and a one-bedroom apartment cannot be overpriced because of the demands of the market. If it costs $1.00 to bring a pear to market then you can charge me $1.10.

The second part of the plan is mixing up our approach to the fight. This is to organize against Shadow Joe with our own virtual entities like guilds, unions, brother- and sisterhoods, special-interest organizations, and watch-groups. We can organize just as well as they can. We can come together and consolidate our wealth. You don't like unions? Okay. Join a special-interest group that fights for your cause. You like to meet our opponent head to head? Create or join a third party that the sold-out politicians *have* to recognize.

If you want to fight the champions of Cost you have to go to the gym to get in shape, you need trainers and other fighters in your corner, you need to organize and to demand a fair shake in the open market. You need room to breathe, time to consider, and a sympathetic and understanding version of your story on the front page of the newspaper.

# UNDERSTANDING
# YOUR WORTH

This step develops from the section on Cost. Worth comes in two forms for the worker and Denizen-wanting-to-be-Citizen. The first of these forms relates to labor and the open market. We work and create products and then buy those products to live and prosper. As I have said above, there need to be certain controls over the Costs of those products which are essential for our survival and well-being.

But this is only the beginning.

We are all potential citizens of the United States of America. We are descended from many generations of workers who built this nation, its cities, corporations, great works, and art. The ground beneath our feet and the sky above our heads belong to us. As far as we can see in any direction this is our country, our nation.

New citizens inherit this property by making their oath and changing their allegiance. We are all equal in this great nation and it, equally, belongs to all of us.

I'm not talking about private property here. Your home is your own. Ford Motors owns their property. This is not a class revolution but merely the recognition of the worth of a nation and its individual members, owners.

Not long ago there was a lot of talk about America's trillions-of-dollars debt to China. News reports and op-ed heads were intimating that, in some way, China owned America. This seemed odd to me. I began to wonder what the full value of our nation was if a foreign country could buy us. Was eight trillion dollars enough?

From there I opened my mind to the vastness that is the United States: the natural resources such as gold, copper, marble, uranium, zinc, precious and semi-precious stones, granite, coal, oil, and natural gas to name just a few; then there's the flora and fauna that fill our wild and tamed areas—deer and steers, coyotes and redwoods, pines, poplars, maples, and arable farmlands, bees and hummingbirds, homing pigeons, and all the fish in our seas, rivers, and lakes; there are the flowing rivers themselves, the electric power that sits dormant in most of them, and the wind and the solar power of the daylight on our brows; there's the labor in our muscles and the content of our minds, libraries, museums, opera houses, and even jails; there are dams and roads and airfields and quays; there are thousands of government and military installations and parks so vast that it takes a day to traverse them; there are the colleges and universities, trade and grade schools; there's water itself and the power of our minds to harness the atom.

Just how much is America worth? And how much of that almost incalculable value belongs to me—Denizen #344,562,891?

How much am I worth? If my government can barter with my inheritance, why can't I? If the complete value of America is 4,127 quadrillion dollars, then why can't I barter with my little portion of that?

Don't get me wrong. I'm not saying that we should sell our country but I am saying that certain questions necessarily arise when we begin to talk about our value, our worth.

For instance: If I, Denizen #344,562,891, am worth 1.9 million dollars, and each member of my family is worth the same, then why can't I send my kids to college, pay my mortgage, afford health insurance, retire when I reach the age of sixty-five (or thirty-two), or just buy a decent rib-eye steak now and again?

This is a valid question. The Congress can make deals with the value of our nation. Big corporations get special rates on mineral rights. China owns a large chunk of our debt. Why can't I afford basic needs if I'm so rich? Why can't we nationalize something like coal or natural gas? Maybe if I felt that the wealth of the oceans was shared a little with me I'd be more likely to worry about its ecological welfare. Why am I kept away from my heritage and my wealth?

This step in personal recovery is more an action of the mind than a direct political economic move. I mean, certainly, there are ways to garner our wealth but first we must imagine our vast value and push aside the notion that this land belongs to someone else. This land is my land, this land is your land . . . that's a fact. Once you accept this reality you will find that you are better able to argue for yourself and your family and friends.

What do you mean I can't have the drugs for my cancer? I'm worth millions. Keep your insurance, your Medicare—give me what I'm worth.

# DEFINING, AND THEN CLAIMING, GENIUS

**M**ost positions of power, influence, and importance in America seem to be out of reach of the Everyday Denizen. There are the Forbes 500, movie stars, political leaders of all stripes, and generals leading the vast armies of the volunteer poor. We live in a world of closed doors, secret headquarters, vaults, closed files, and covert actions. There are plots and counterplots, hidden enemies and terrorists who live up to their name even though they go undetected and seemingly take no action.

It seems as if we, the People, cannot seriously affect this world of secrecy and concentrated power. We cast our votes but the decisions that are made by our leaders remain unchanged. We do our jobs and are still laid off. We feel love in our hearts but still find ourselves alone.

And when hearing about the billionaires, film directors, and presidents speak to us we are often told, by their second and third tiers of acolytes, that they are geniuses.

*Leave him alone*, they say, *he knows what he's doing.*

This phrase says two things: first, that the leader has Knowledge and, second, that we, the People, do not.

This is not a partisan argument. I'm not talking about Democrat versus Republican. I'm simply saying that the majority of our experts, leaders, and specialists over the past century have served to wound the world not heal it. Millions upon millions have died, have suffered torture, have been raped and sodomized, have been turned into killer soldiers at the ages of six and seven. With all the pomp and genius and holy secrets, the poor and moderately intelligent suffer in ignorance.

I take the above statements as facts. It requires an act of evil genius to slaughter six million in the camps, to murder a million people a year in a twenty-nine-year reign of terror, to starve and otherwise kill fifty million in the paroxysm of decades that culminated in the Cultural Revolution. It takes a concert of minds in malevolent concord to maintain revolutions and covert military acts in Asia, South America, the Middle East, and Africa from the '50s until today.

Yes, he might be a genius, but so what? What makes a genius good or right or on my side? Indeed, how can a genius even exist without us? Could Mozart have made himself a violin at the age of two or twenty-two? No. Could Einstein have expressed his theories without the language in his head that had been forming for millennia? No.

We, the People, are the genius. We are repositories of thousands of years of language, wisdom, and hard knocks. When we come together in a sublime cultural epiphany: That's when there is potential and growth.

The old man, who has forgotten much, holding the young boy's hand and leading him to a lake of wonder that he knows: This is the potential for genius.

We need to know, like Socrates knew, that we are ignorant in the extreme and only through dialogue and respect for others can we begin to cobble out an understanding of the truth.

There might have been a different outcome if, before he stood in front of the assembled UN and damned Iraq, Colin Powell had shown us the yellow dots in the desert that his nameless experts claimed were weapons of mass destruction. Felicia Saunders from Cleveland, Ohio, might have spoken up and asked if there was any possibility that they could have been something else. Paolo Ein in Memphis, Tennessee, who has worked with septic tanks his whole life, might have come forward and said that he had seen aerial pictures of septic tanks that looked disturbingly similar. Ben Barcelona in East New York might have asked why one country could have such weapons but others could not? And Beverly Chin of Santa Monica, California, might have wondered if, even if these dots were WMDs, we might do a surgical strike against the dots and not the people of an entire nation.

This dialogue is genius despite Colin Powell's IQ. We, the People, are the genius. We, together, make up the mind, heart, and conscience of America. All these secrets and last-minute claims have nothing to with brilliance, leadership, or morality. Powell was wrong but, worse, we were wrong for listening to him. We have been disassociated by a system of separation of labor (defined by the Joes) and then considered only when we have something to say about our little corner of expertise. We are effectively cut off from the mainstream of decision-making by experts who owe their bread and butter and jam and caviar to the Joes. And these Joes aren't worried about collateral damage or an eight-year-old girl being gang-raped by a troop of Congolese mercenaries. They have cell phones to move and Venezuela to reacquire.

The individual geniuses and the Joes are brutes and thugs who believe that they are right because they can get around us. And they will continue to get around us if we don't start demanding truth from our leaders and a willingness to listen too. Without our input and our experience, the experts' genius is nullified. Without collaboration politics becomes a high-stakes game where there have to be winners and losers—and the losers are almost always us.

So what should we do to pit our communal genius against their false claims?

Get together with a dozen people and ask a question, any question that brings to light a cultural or political conundrum. Let each member of the twelve make a brief comment on how they see the problem and what they think might be a solution[*]—all this in statements as simple and short as possible. Do not argue about the claims but allow questions to be asked about the assumptions, the expected consequences, and the unexpected turns these definitions and answers might bring about. Do this all in a pleasant setting with food, maybe a little wine on the table. You might let the individual members of this group alternate as the secretary who puts everything down so that later on the members can go over their discussion.

This weekly, bi-weekly, or monthly meeting will be an exercise in genius. No one will pay you for this conference. If someone offers to pay you—turn them down. If a joke comes to mind—tell it. If you have an unpopular opinion, speak it. In many sessions, maybe most of them, you will not come to an agreement but this is all right; the exercise of thinking outside the coffin-like box the Joes have built for you will open your heart to the confidence of participatory leadership. That is what America needs.

We all have a piece of the puzzle. Genius is a collaborative phenomenon. Yes, there are some amazing minds in the world but these minds are all just small

---

[*] If, indeed, they think a solution is possible.

pieces of the Great Soul that we inhabit. The mere fact that someone adds faster or sees deeper does not mean that she doesn't need the trace elements of others' knowledge. And intelligence comes in all kinds of packages.

The exercise of the Meeting of the Twelve will help its members to begin to see the possibilities in us while at the same time reinforcing the notion of how cut off we've been from the real decision-making going on in our lives.

Coming together and discussing, digesting the opinions of our peers, readdressing issues and going over the possible answers again—these are the methods we must use to pass judgment on the modern world. We are the juries that must decide what crimes have been committed, what punishments must be meted out, and what payments must be made to make right what has been done wrong.

# AFTERWORD

This short monograph has been designed to question the assumptions of and about our so-called leadership and to offer some alternative ways of thinking about the world that we have been tumbled into. There are probably many more steps that we need to take in order to arrive at a bus stop where there's a place for everyone, but this is a beginning. We start by defining ourselves and the inhospitable environment that encompasses us; then we take small, human steps to counter our vast opponents. Not to worry—viruses are the smallest life-form we know of but they can fell the greatest of beasts. We need to become viral, to have many meetings of

The Twelve, to join unions and exercise real democratic processes. We need to define a twenty-first-century education and tell the truth at least once a day. We need to define *class*, place ourselves within that definition, and make our allegiances accordingly. Maybe we could benefit from the tool of psychotherapy and definitely we should work on our political convictions every day. We must resurrect the democratic process and come to an understanding of how the economic infrastructure creates our minds. We must know what the Cost of living in this world actually is—and also the value of our labors. We have to understand what we're worth as people and as citizens of this great land and, consequently, we need to see our interconnectedness as a kind of genius that trumps any Harvard grad or wealthy wannabe.

I believe that these steps will lead to others and that—as thousands and millions of us begin to tramp toward the goal of truth, liberation, and equality—a road shall appear beneath our feet that the rest of the world will have to follow.